THE JUNIOR WITCH'S HANDBOOK

THE JUNIOR WITCH'S HANDBOOK

A Kid's Guide to White Magic, Spells, and Rituals

NIKKI VAN DE CAR

Illustrations by **UTA KROGMANN**

RP | KIDS
PHILADELPHIA

Running Press Kids
Hachette Book Group
1290 Avenue of the Americas, New York, NY 10104
www.runningpress.com/rpkids
@RP_Kids

Printed in China

First Edition: June 2020

Published by Running Press Kids, an imprint of Perseus Books, LLC,
a subsidiary of Hachette Book Group, Inc. The Running Press Kids name
and logo is a trademark of the Hachette Book Group.

The Hachette Speakers Bureau provides a wide range of authors for speaking events.
To find out more, go to www.hachettespeakersbureau.com or call (866) 376-6591.

The publisher is not responsible for websites (or their content)
that are not owned by the publisher.

Print book cover and interior design by Frances J. Soo Ping Chow
Stock illustrations page. ii: GettyImages/Utro_na_more

Library of Congress Control Number: 2019948852

ISBNs: 978-0-7624-6930-7 (hardcover), 978-0-7624-6931-4 (ebook)

1010

10   9   8   7   6   5

For:

MAILE

MY FAVORITE,
NOT-SO-JUNIOR WITCH

CONTENTS

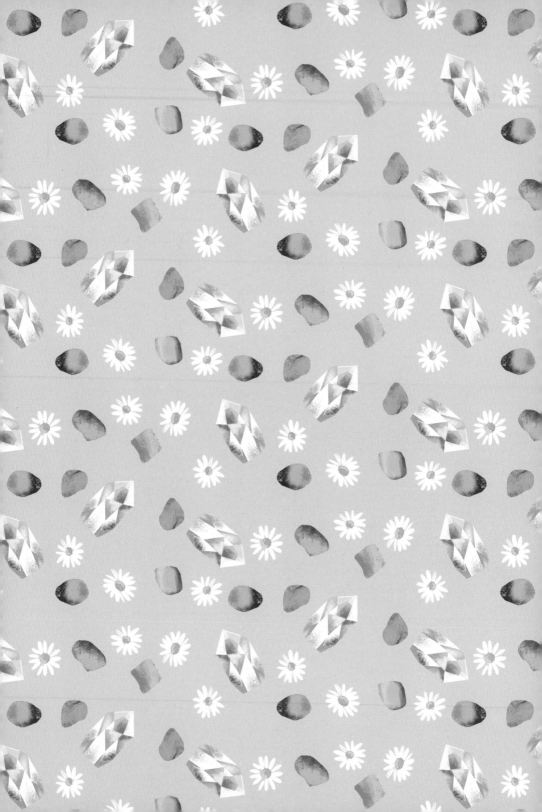

INTRODUCTION

If you only associate witchcraft with pointy black hats, ugly moles, flying on broomsticks, and putting curses on innocent children, think again.

If you think it's all pretend, you're wrong about that, too.

The history of witchcraft is made up of powerful women, but maybe not in the way you think. Sure, there are stories of the witches of Salem calling down curses, but that isn't really what it was all about. Witchcraft was often misunderstood, and wise women or hedge witches who provided natural healing remedies and support for childbirth were accused of some pretty crazy things, like killing pigs or hexing cotton—likely because those whose pigs or cotton died in a blight wanted someone to blame. In reality, witchcraft has always been about caring for the earth and caring for those who dwell here.

And that certainly isn't done with creepy rituals or calling on any demons! Magic is essentially good, and it's all based on something incredibly simple: intention. If you mean for something to be true, then it is. If you chant a spell, but you don't actually believe in it or really put your soul into it, then nothing will happen. But you can stand there and say nothing at all and really *feel* what you want to create, and that can be the most powerful magic of all. It all comes from you.

So, obviously, that can work both ways. We certainly have the power to intend for something bad to happen, but a witch knows better, because she is bound by something called The Rule of Three. This rule, which is essentially a law of the universe, declares that anything we put forth into the world will be returned upon us, threefold. So you can see why, in practice, all magic is white magic!

There is magic all around us, and it is created *by us* and *for us*. It is in the air we breathe and the ground on which we walk, in the space between what we wish were true and what we *make* true. Accessing this magic requires imagination, creativity, a connection with the earth, and, most of all, a sense of curiosity and possibility within your heart.

This handbook is just a guide to get you started on your journey to becoming a witch. You'll learn the basics of herb magic, crystals, ritual magic, and meditation magic, but the spells and potions included here are just a way for you to begin your practice so that you can expand it from there, creating your own spells and your own rituals, as you grow into your powers.

The book is organized into three sections: Friends, Fulfillment, and Family, the three areas of our lives that have the most impact on us and that require the most of us. Within those sections are three categories of spellwork: Creating, Healing, and Empowering, and each category includes at least one spell and meditation.

Creation magic always has to come at the beginning, for obvious reasons—without it, we would be nowhere! In Creating, you'll be asking questions of yourself—what is it that you want in a friend, in your life, in your home? And then you'll get to work making it happen.

Because life isn't perfect (and is therefore so much more interesting), it's important to practice healing magic in all of these areas. People hurt us, and we hurt them—it's part of being in this world and interacting with those around us. Knowing how to heal from those hurts, and to help others do so, is at the core of any witch's practice.

The final category of each section, Empowering, will help you remember who you are and what you are capable of. It will help you shed any limitations you might think you have and fully step into your power—power that is your birthright, has been passed on through generations of women, and is yours to claim.

Keep track of everything you do in your own magic notebook. In witchy terms, this is called a *grimoire*. Sometimes you may not have the ingredients you need for a particular spell on hand, and that's okay! You can make any substitutions you like, and just keep track of them in your grimoire. The Table of Correspondences on page xx will help you come up with any replacements you might need.

For now, take a deep breath and close your eyes. Let's work some magic.

THINGS YOU'LL NEED

Altar

An altar is a place to focus your thoughts and energies, in either very specific or very general ways, depending on what's going on in your life at that moment.

Your room is probably the best place for your altar, either in the corner on the floor or on your dresser or bedside table. It doesn't need to be very big.

Start with the basics: First, what is going to be your central symbol? It can be a photograph or some other image of someone you love, an ancestor, or even a goddess. You could use a bowl or chalice if you want to focus on inviting positive energies into your life, or an incense burner if you want to disperse negative energies. You could use a large, powerful crystal—anything that feels right. This kind of magic is very personal and very dependent on your own intuition. And remember, your decision is not final—this is just what your altar will look like today. You can change it around anytime you want to.

You may also want to incorporate the elements. Here are some possibilities:

FIRE

candle

volcanic stones

incense

AIR

feather

essential oil diffuser

eggshells

WATER

seashell

a mirror

jar of rainwater

EARTH

horn or bone

sedimentary rock

pottery

From here, get creative and have fun with it! Add things to your altar and remove them when they no longer feel right. You can include things you find, like buttons or lost keys, pieces of friendship bracelets, essential oils, bits of cloth, crystals, dried herbs— anything and everything you want.

When you're working on a big spell or focusing your energy toward something you really want, spend a little time with your altar, rearranging it and redecorating it. It'll help you align your desires with your power.

Crystals

Certain rocks, gems, and minerals have been used in healing and magic for 6,000 years, dating back to ancient Egypt. Different stones have different uses and abilities. For instance, diamonds have the ability to draw out poison, garnet to protect from nightmares, opal to boost creativity, and lapis lazuli to enhance mystical powers.

It can get really complicated! There are *a lot* of different kinds of rocks out there, and their uses can overlap and complement one another. The way we use them also depends on their size and shape:

CHUNK CRYSTAL. This includes geodes, pyrite, turquoise, or any kind of untouched crystal that looks basically the same way it did when it came out of the earth. These are often viewed as really useful knickknacks—you would keep them around your desk or in your room, providing your space with clarity, peace, protection, or whatever that particular crystal is best known for.

CUT CRYSTAL. Diamonds and other gems used in jewelry are cut to enhance their sparkle and capture light. They are very pretty, and often very powerful, as their impurities have been trimmed away.

TUMBLED. These are the stones you can often find in bins at a science or mystical shop. They're softer, often rounded, and likely to be the crystals you use most in your daily magic practice.

WAND. This type is of crystal is shaped a bit like a literal wand, so that it's pointy at one end. You will find these useful in targeting the crystal's energies. In particular, a selenium or clear quartz wand is used to activate a crystal grid.

Your stones will require some care and feeding! They work by taking on and releasing energy, but that means that you need to clear those energies and then recharge your crystals fairly often. Do this as soon as you purchase a stone, clearing any energies it may have picked up along its way to you, and then repeat that process once it's been used, so that it's ready for the next time you need it.

CLEARING. You can do this in a number of ways! You can wave a smudge stick over it (see page 78) or soak it in salt water overnight.

You can hold it in a stream or in the rain, or you can let it be washed by sunshine or moonlight.

CHARGING. For general charging, you can simply hold your crystal to your heart or your third eye (on your forehead, right between your eyebrows) and visualize its magic—its protection, its love, its healing. Feel that magic within yourself and within the crystal. Feel that interplay between the two of you. Then, gently place the crystal wherever it is you keep it, knowing that it is ready for you whenever you need it. However, if you want to program your crystal with something specific, say for instance healing a sore throat, rather than general healing, this is best done right before your ritual or spell. You'll follow the same process as above, but focus your intention—if you're using rose quartz, for instance, what specific love are you looking to enhance?

Herbs

There are two kinds of herb magic. The first is the more obvious one, the one we do every day without thinking about it. When you're feeling a little stressed, you drink a cup of chamomile tea. When you need a bit of a boost, you might chew some peppermint gum. When your stomach is upset, you drink some ginger ale. This is everyday magic, employing herbs and plants that are so powerful we have grown used to turning to them without thinking about it.

The second form of herb magic feels much witchier. This is where we use herbs not just for healing, but to enhance the power and energy of our spells. Like crystals, certain herbs have certain properties and can be applied to amplify our own abilities.

Often herbs are used in a gris-gris, or a small bag that can be used as a talisman (see page 2). You can also consume some of the herbs as tea—lavender is delicious, mugwort not so much—so that your body is prepared for your ritual. Check to make sure the herb is edible first, though!

You can also create a smudge stick to use before conducting a spell or ritual. A smudge stick is a small bundle of dried plants that you light on fire to activate their specific virtues. To create a smudge stick, collect the fresh or dried herbs of your choice, and lay them together into a bundle about five inches long and maybe an inch or two thick. Wind cotton string or yarn tightly around your bundle, moving up and down the length of the stems, until you have a nice tight stick. If you've used fresh plants, you'll need to hang your smudge stick to dry for at least a week before using.

When it's ready, light the tip of your smudge stick, but then blow it out so it's just smoldering—you don't need a licking flame. Wave your smudge stick over a crystal grid or around the space where you'll be casting your spell, or let it rest on a dish and allow its smoke to move through you.

Essential Oils

You'll notice that sometimes a spell will call for the same plant in either herb or essential oil form. The truth is that both are equally powerful, but have different uses. Essential oils are a distilled version of the plant; they capture its aroma as well as its magical properties—literally its "essence." So it would take a handful of dried lavender to achieve the same power as a drop of lavender essential oil. Also, a number of the essential oils we'll be using are hard to find in fresh or dried form! When's the last time you saw myrrh or frankincense at the supermarket?

Now, you don't need all of the recommended oils. There are a lot of sources for essential oils out there, and some of them are *really* pricey. You don't need those.

Look for therapeutic-grade oil, but don't stress about how highly rated it is. But no matter what, don't ever drink your essential oils! Even essential oils made from herbs we normally eat, like sage or thyme, can be toxic because they are so very intense. Some of them, like lemon or lime, shouldn't be used directly on your skin, while others like chamomile or rose are gentle enough and can even be good for your skin, which is a nice bonus. More often, though, you'll use your essential oils to anoint candles or crystals.

Table of Correspondences

If you don't have all the ingredients you need for a particular spell, this table will help you substitute a different crystal, herb, or essential oil. If you don't have any of the herbs, you could just work in a crystal—remember, this is *your* spell, and you get to decide how it works!

LIFE SKILL	HERBS	CRYSTALS	ESSENTIAL OILS
Balance	Alyssum, sunflower, lavender	Clear quartz, moonstone, pearl	Cedarwood, geranium, lavender
Boundaries	Hawthorn, yarrow, basil	Tiger's-eye, pyrite, hematite	Basil, neroli, palo santo
Communication	Mint, parsley, yarrow	Aquamarine, blue calcite, blue apatite	Lavender, sage, neroli
Compassion	Marjoram, angelica, rose, hibiscus, violet	Rose quartz, malachite, jade, green aventurine	Rose, bergamot
Concentration	Rosemary, mint, sage, cinnamon	Amethyst, lapis lazuli, smoky quartz	Frankincense, myrrh, rosemary, lemon
Confidence	Fennel, motherwort, sunflower	Pyrite, yellow jasper, tiger's-eye, citrine	ginger, lemon
Courage	Black cohosh, garlic, yarrow, Saint-John's-wort	Amber, carnelian, garnet, red jasper	Myrrh, cinnamon, palo santo, sweet orange
Creativity	Tomato, vervain, ylang-ylang	Opal, garnet, carnelian	Jasmine, sandalwood
Divination	Holly, marigold, mugwort, wormwood	Opal, moonstone, lapis lazuli, amethyst	Lavender, rosemary, frankincense

Energy	Allspice, cinnamon, lime, lemon	Calcite, citrine, clear quartz, jade, opal, tiger's-eye	Ginger, lemon, lime, sweet orange
Friendship	Crocus, evening primrose, cardamom	Rose quartz, malachite, green aventurine	Rose, bergamot, ginger
Harmony	Basil, marjoram, lemon balm	Carnelian, malachite, clear quartz	Rose, bergamot, lavender
Healing	Allspice, aloe, cinnamon, violet	Amethyst, clear quartz, turquoise, obsidian	Angelica, cloves, lavender
Intuition	Goldenrod, eyebright, yarrow	Amazonite, lapis lazuli, smoky quartz	Lavender, frankincense, myrrh
Luck	Allspice, clover, almond, cinquefoil	Agate, amazonite, amber, moonstone, peridot	Mint, cloves
Meditation	Acacia, anise, chamomile	Calcite, obsidian, amethyst, lapis lazuli	Frankincense, lavender, myrrh
Peace	Alyssum, basil, violet, chamomile, lemon balm	Moonstone, rose quartz, turquoise, hematite, azurite, aquamarine	Lavender, rose, chamomile
Protection	Yarrow, basil, parsley	Hematite, smoky quartz, obsidian	Palo santo, pine, neroli
Rest	Lemon balm, vervain, yarrow, rue	Amethyst, clear quartz, malachite, moonstone	Lavender, chamomile
Strength	Garlic, mint, parsley, thyme	Fossil, garnet, hematite	Pine, tea tree oil, sweet orange
Wisdom	Apple, hazel, vervain	Amethyst, lapis lazuli, clear quartz	Sage, lavender, rosemary

FRIENDSHIP

Our friends can often be the most important people in our lives. They laugh with us, cry with us, support us, and teach us.

Part of what makes them so special to us is that we have *chosen* them. It's such an incredible thing, when you think about it—out of all the people you know, you have found these three or four people (or ten or twelve, if you're the outgoing sort!) that really get you, that you can really connect with. You have so much in common, whether it's similar tastes in books and TV shows or just a way of looking at the world.

You chose them, and they chose you.

There is power in that choice—but power always goes two ways. You can be incredibly close with your friends, but still have moments when, whether intentional or not, they hurt your feelings or you hurt theirs.

Friendships require care, thoughtfulness, and intention—but if you put the necessary work in, you can have a relationship that is meaningful, supportive, and so much fun.

Creating

SPELL TO
INVITE NEW FRIENDSHIP

• • • • • •

This spell can come in handy when you've moved to another town, another school, or if you just feel like there's a gap somewhere—that you've got an interest your other friends don't share and it would be great to have someone to enjoy it with!

Start by taking a piece of paper and writing down the characteristics you're looking for in this new friendship. Do you want someone who is imaginative? Someone who is into music? Someone who likes karate? Is this person going to be kind, outgoing, studious, hilarious? Write it all down, then fold your piece of paper up nice and small.

Create a gris-gris bag by cutting a two- or three-inch square of cloth. Choose your cloth carefully—do you want something soft or sparkly? What color feels right? Follow your intuition here, as you think about the kind of friend you want to invite into your life.

Place the piece of paper on the cloth. If you want, you can add some rose quartz or malachite and sprinkle the cloth with a bit of rose or ginger essential oil. Bring the edges together and tie it up with a ribbon. Make sure it's nice and tight.

For the next three nights, sleep with the bag beneath your pillow or next to your heart so that your unconscious mind can work its powers.

You should know, though, that your new friend may show up in unexpected ways. You may find that you meet *exactly* the person you envisioned right after those three nights' sleep, or it may take a while longer. You might even find that an old friend, someone you've known forever, is suddenly different, more exciting—as if they suddenly are all the things you were looking for when you worked your spell.

RITUAL TO CONNECT WITH MAMA EARTH
AND WITH EACH OTHER

•• • •• •

Friends support each other, but sometimes friendship itself needs a little support. By connecting with that which literally holds us up in space—the earth—we can create a foundation for our friendship that will hold strong, whatever quakes or storms may come.

Pick a nice, sunny day, because you'll definitely want to be outside for this. Find a patch of grass, anywhere you can really get down low and touch the earth itself, with nothing between you. Sit in a circle with your friends—it can be just two of you or as many as you like! You'll want to sit cross-legged, so that your knees are touching.

Lay your palms on either side of you, flat on the earth. Place your hands so that your fingertips touch those of your friends. Now, breathe together. Inhale for a count of four, hold for a count of two, and exhale for a count of six. Repeat these breaths two times for each participant.

Seal the ritual by clasping hands and bowing your heads. Thank one another for the support each of you gives the other. Thank Mama Earth for supporting us all.

WITCHY CODES

While we know now that witchcraft is a loving, light-filled way to connect with our personal power, we also know that it isn't always viewed that way. It certainly wasn't back in the days of the Salem witch trials, and even today some people might think witchcraft is a little weird or spooky.

Once witchcraft became equated with paganism and therefore rejected by the Church, witches needed to disguise themselves, to hide who they were and what they did in order to avoid persecution. But that didn't mean their services weren't still required! So what had been an honored profession and service in the community became something whispered about among the women of the village, with their knowledge passed down in secret.

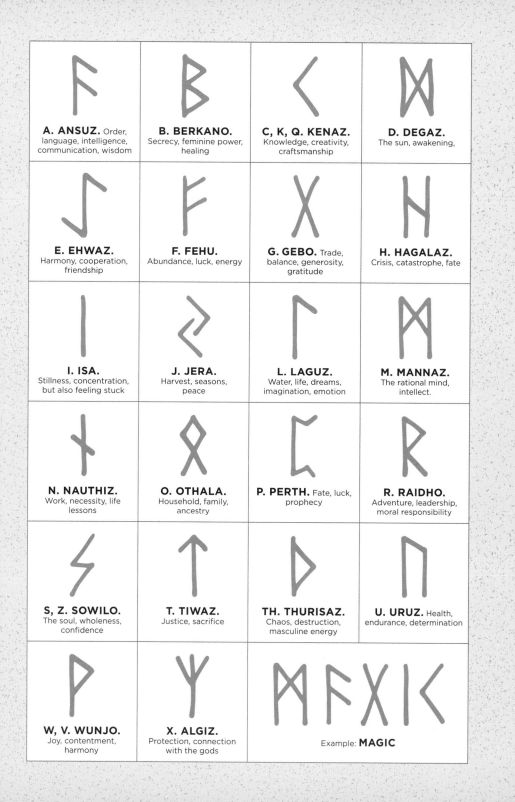

A. ANSUZ. Order, language, intelligence, communication, wisdom

B. BERKANO. Secrecy, feminine power, healing

C, K, Q. KENAZ. Knowledge, creativity, craftsmanship

D. DEGAZ. The sun, awakening,

E. EHWAZ. Harmony, cooperation, friendship

F. FEHU. Abundance, luck, energy

G. GEBO. Trade, balance, generosity, gratitude

H. HAGALAZ. Crisis, catastrophe, fate

I. ISA. Stillness, concentration, but also feeling stuck

J. JERA. Harvest, seasons, peace

L. LAGUZ. Water, life, dreams, imagination, emotion

M. MANNAZ. The rational mind, intellect.

N. NAUTHIZ. Work, necessity, life lessons

O. OTHALA. Household, family, ancestry

P. PERTH. Fate, luck, prophecy

R. RAIDHO. Adventure, leadership, moral responsibility

S, Z. SOWILO. The soul, wholeness, confidence

T. TIWAZ. Justice, sacrifice

TH. THURISAZ. Chaos, destruction, masculine energy

U. URUZ. Health, endurance, determination

W, V. WUNJO. Joy, contentment, harmony

X. ALGIZ. Protection, connection with the gods

Example: **MAGIC**

This kind of secrecy isn't necessary nowadays, but it *is* kind of fun and a way of honoring those witches who had to live and practice in secret.

One way to dabble in a little secrecy is to develop a system of codes, so that you and your friends can discuss your magic without anyone else knowing. You can devise your own system, with certain agreed upon symbols. For instance, you could have an apple representing the letter "A" and so forth.

Or you can use a dead language that nobody knows how to read! The Elder Futhark is a set of Nordic runes that date back to the eighth century. The word *rune* means "holding a secret," and runes were believed to be so powerful that they could only be understood and used by the wise and brave. They were often carved into stones or tiles and used for divination, or to understand what the right thing to do might be in a given situation. So, if you were a Viking chieftain and you needed to decide whether to venture forth on a new exploration, you would consult with your Erilaz (sorcerer advisor) who would cast the runes and interpret them to determine the best course of action. They were also used as talismans, to bring their meaning to the person carrying them or wearing them.

They represent a variety of concepts, but they can also be used in place of letters. You can use them as a simple letter-replacement code, and no one will ever be able to guess what you're saying!

TEA RITUAL

• • ● • •

This ritual is inspired by both afternoon tea parties with stuffed animals (throwback!) and an ancient Japanese tea ceremony called The Way of Tea.

Even if you weren't the tea party type growing up, this ritual will evoke that sense of play and imagination—of sheer, childish fun. But it is also quite serious. The Way of Tea is a ceremony that dates back to the ninth century, and it is taught at schools in tea clubs. If done properly (and that's no easy feat!), a Japanese tea ceremony will provide not just relaxed communication between the host and guests, but deep spiritual satisfaction.

Since you don't have years of studying The Way of Tea under your belt, we're going to lower our expectations a little bit and aim for pleasure and fun.

Start by treating this ceremony as an event. Send out invitations, and invite everyone to get dressed up. Plan your menu carefully, including several options for snacks and treats. Consider your guests' needs above all else—who is coming? What do they like to eat? Traditionally we would serve green tea, but an herbal tea will work just as well.

Unlike your previous tea parties, we won't be using pretty teacups, at least not to start. The tea will be brewed and served in a single ceramic bowl. Once your tea has steeped, offer the bowl to a friend with a bow. Your friend should bow in return, and then rotate the bowl, taking a sip from the edge that had been farthest away from them. Your friend should then repeat this process with the next guest, and so on, ending with the host, until everyone has had a sip of tea from the bowl.

From there, everyone can relax a bit. The serious part of the ritual has been completed. You have honored your guests and brought forth a sense of harmony, tranquility, and peace. Now you can shift into chatting, snacking, and sipping tea—from cups if you like!—at your leisure.

Healing

MEDITATION FOR ANGER

• • • • • •

Sometimes, without meaning to, our friends can cross a line. They can be hurtful, they can be demanding, and we can feel that we are giving more than we are receiving.

This doesn't necessarily make them a bad friend—in fact, often, they have absolutely no idea they are hurting us until we lash out at them. It can start with something really small, like loaning a book. It's a book you love, one that you really want your friend to read and enjoy! And she loved it, too—until she lost it.

Okay, these things happen. But then she wants to borrow a sweater. Of course, you don't want her to be cold! But then she gets paint on it. You tell her it's fine, not to worry. But then something similar happens, over and over, until you feel like she doesn't care about you, if she's treating your stuff this way.

Now let's think about it from her perspective. She probably guesses you didn't like that sweater that much anyway, if you didn't care that she got paint on it. She certainly hasn't been keeping track of how many things of yours she's lost or ruined, because she just hasn't realized it bothered you—because you didn't tell her.

And then she loses one thing too many, and *you* lose it and yell at her about it. And now she's hurt and angry, too, because for her, this is coming out of nowhere and feels like a giant overreaction.

We've all been in these kinds of situations, on both sides. The way to avoid them is to react sooner, before you're upset. One lost book? No big deal. But after a few things, it's time to say something, even if you're not angry about it yet. Otherwise, she won't know she's doing something that bothers you.

The tricky part, sometimes, can be realizing that it bothers you before you're angry! But here's the thing—many times, you *are* angry, you just don't realize it or want to pay attention to it. This makes sense, because anger isn't a fun emotion to feel. But it's there, and often it's trying to tell you something important.

This meditation practice will help you tune in to that early anger, that anger you may not even know you're feeling, so that you can hear what it's trying to say and act on it before it starts shouting at you—and making you shout at other people.

On a day when your friend has bothered you, but you don't really want to think it's a big deal (and it isn't, not yet) find a quiet space, somewhere without distractions. Sit comfortably and hold some tiger's-eye or pyrite in your nondominant hand, palm closed around it. (That's your left hand if you're right-handed, your right hand if you're left-handed.) Now, tune in to what you're feeling. It's okay, it can't harm anyone. Even though you told your friend you weren't bothered, ask yourself: are you bothered?

Now ask yourself *what exactly* bothers you. In a story like the ruined stuff, it's not really the *stuff* that's the issue, it's the sense that if your friend cares so little for your things, how much does she really care about you? You may fight against exploring this feeling, because you do know, in so many other ways, how good a friend she is. But allowing yourself to feel this emotion doesn't change that; you can know that she's a good friend and have hurt feelings at the same time.

In this space of knowing your friend cares about you *and* knowing that she's not doing a great job of showing it in this instance, find your balance between the two. Get comfortable with it. Breathe slowly in and out, allowing yourself to find peace.

When you feel nice and relaxed, open your eyes. What you've done here is taken the emotion, the anger and hurt, out of the situation. Now you can calmly tell your friend, "Hey, I want you to take better care of my stuff" without being angry and without feeling hurt. That way, she can hear what you're saying without getting angry herself. And it'll stay no big deal.

MEDITATION FOR COMPASSION

• • ● • •

Sometimes, though, our friends drive us crazy, and there's nothing we can do about it. They're distant, they're angry at us when we haven't done anything (from our perspective, anyway), they're mean for no reason, or they're just really annoying.

This happens. Nobody is perfect all the time. Maybe you're on the other side of the ruined stuff situation and you just don't realize it, or maybe they've got some drama going on that you don't know about. It doesn't make it right that they're treating you this way, but they are and you can't *make* them behave differently.

All you can do is try to be compassionate and support them (maybe from afar, if they're being really unpleasant) while they go through whatever it is that's bothering them. This isn't easy! But this meditation can help you find the empathy and compassion you need to be a good friend, even if you're the only one who's being good right now. *Mettā* or loving-kindess is a meditation practice that has ancient roots, from even before Buddha walked the earth.

Sit comfortably. Hold some rose quartz or malachite in your nondominant hand, palm closed. Close your eyes and take a few deep breaths. Start by tuning in to your own feelings—are you hurt? Angry? Annoyed? These are valid, and you need to allow yourself to feel this way. Be kind to yourself here. If you want, you can think to yourself, "May I be happy. May I be peaceful. May I be free from suffering."

Now, turn your thoughts to your friend. Are they angry? Hurt? Annoyed? Probably, if they're treating you this way. You know from experience that those feelings are really painful. You don't wish them on yourself or on your friend. Send the kindness you have for yourself outward, thinking of your friend. "May you be happy. May you be peaceful. May you be free from suffering."

Open your palm to let your energy and good wishes flow out of you. Repeat "May you be happy. May you be peaceful. May you be free from suffering." You'll find that tomorrow, you're more patient and less likely to get your feelings hurt by your friend's behavior. And soon enough, thanks to your compassion, your friend will be back to her usual kind, fun self.

HEALING SPELL TO LET GO
OF HURT FEELINGS

• • ● • •

Unfortunately, it isn't always that easy. Sometimes, whether they mean to or not, our friends can hurt us so deeply that a little meditation doesn't really fix it. Sometimes we've hurt them. This spell can help heal that wound in your friendship. It's something you can do on your own or, if you're ready, with your friend, so that you can heal each other.

Timing is important here. A spell won't work unless you *want* it to, so there's no point in trying it unless you are really ready to let go of your hurt feelings and mend the friendship. You might want to try meditating on your emotions first, to see what you're truly feeling.

If you decide you're ready, gather some amethyst, clear quartz, violets, and salt. If you don't have all of these, no worries—you can work with what you have. Place or sprinkle just enough to create a sacred circle large enough to hold you.

Sit inside the circle. Close your eyes, and let yourself really feel all that anger, all that hurt. This is the last time you're going to be feeling it, so let it in. And then—let it out. Visualize breathing in new air, a fresh start, and breathing out all of that hurt, all of that anger. That hurt is held by the sacred circle, and it is fine for it to be there.

When you feel like you've gotten it all out, open your eyes. Come to your feet, and step outside of the circle. From the outside, take apart the circle, collecting your crystals and herbs, allowing the feelings trapped in there to blow away. You may still have some lingering anger, to be honest—there's no magic that can make it go away entirely—but now it will be easier to deal with and it will eventually be forgotten.

GRIS-GRIS TO
MAINTAIN CONNECTION

• • • • • •

Sometimes the separation we feel from our friends can come not from squabbles or annoyances, but from circumstances outside of our control. Someone might move, change schools, or just stop being around as much. It can be very hard when you're no longer able to do the same things together and spend the same kind of time together. It can feel like, no matter how much you want to stay friends, it's all going to fall apart.

There are things you can do to prevent this from happening: regularly scheduled phone calls, get-togethers if possible, text chains—and, of course, magic. This is a project you should work on together and should make for each other. As on page 2, start by choosing fabric. Use your friend's favorite color, and choose a texture that feels right. Cut a four-inch square, and fill it with dried mint, rose quartz, or malachite. Finally, add something special. For example, if your friend is into science, add a drawing of oxytocin, the love molecule. You could create a tiny stuffed animal of their favorite creature. Give it some thought, and choose what feels right, but make it small, so it fits in the gris-gris.

Cut a length of ribbon or twine, close the edges of the gris-gris and tie it tight. Exchange it for the one your friend made for you. Keep yours close, even when your friend is far away.

Empowering

FRIENDSHIP KNOTS

· · ● · · ·

Did you know that friendship bracelets, those things we've all worn and given to each other, are rooted in some of the oldest magic there is? Knot magic is the act of tying literal knots into a cord or a piece of thread and using it to bind a spell. Sailors would use knot magic to bind winds and would untie the knots when they were becalmed or needed an extra boost.

Knot magic is not permanent, as it can be untied—but that's what makes it perfect for friendship magic. Remember, friendship

is a *choice,* one that we make again and again. You and your friends have chosen each other, and these knots can be a symbol of that choice.

Start by picking the right materials. What best represents your friend? Is she into unicorns and sparkles and purple? Then perhaps some spangly yarn would be the way to go. Is your friend more of the adventurous type? Maybe some leather cord would be good. Give it some thought.

Magic often works best in threes, so start by writing down three or six or nine (or some other multiple of three) things you and your friend share. Then take your cord and tie a knot for the first connection you have together, speaking it aloud. You can then string on a bead or anything else that feels right. Then tie the next knot, for the next connection, again speaking it aloud. Repeat until all your knots are in place.

From there, if you want, you can turn your knot magic into a piece of jewelry! If it's small, make it a bracelet, or it can be worn as a necklace. Give it as a gift, as a symbol of your friendship, or get the group together so you make a bunch of them together, for each other!

DIVINATION SPELL

• • ● • •

Divination has two meanings: 1. to look into the future and literally see what's going to happen, and 2. to use your intuition to gain insight into what will happen in the future.

The first one is pretty unlikely, really. There are just too many possibilities in life—every choice you make can lead to hundreds of *new* choices that didn't exist before. That's really exciting, but it does make predicting the future a pretty inexact science.

This divination spell won't give you a winning lottery number or tell you the name of your college roommate. Instead, it will help you look inside yourself, to divine what is right and true for *you*. What do you want to be when you grow up? Which friend should you hang out with this weekend? These are the kinds of questions you should ask when performing this spell.

Start by anointing a candle with lavender or frankincense essential oil—though don't get the wick wet! Place your candle on a small plate, and surround the base with opal, moonstone, or lapis lazuli crystals. If it's available, sprinkle some mugwort or wormwood around your candle, too. Light the candle, and sit so that you are bathed in its light.

Look at the candle and allow your thoughts to drift. Ask yourself, what do I want? Allow your imagination to drift, thinking about what your life *might* be like and what you might desire. Keep going, until the candle reaches the point where it starts to drip.

What were you thinking of at that moment? Write it down, and then wait and see! Perhaps that was your future at that moment, on that day, but it will shift because of a choice you are going to make tomorrow. Or maybe you are spot-on!

CRYSTAL GRID TO DEEPEN
YOUR FRIENDSHIP

• • ● • •

In *Anne of Green Gables,* Anne Shirley wants nothing more than a "bosom friend." Not a regular friend, but a kindred spirit, someone you can trust with your secrets, your dreams, and your innermost self. We all long for that closeness. This crystal grid is intended to help you bridge that gap, bringing a regular friend to a true best friend.

This is something you can do on your own or in a group, and it's really fun—there's something artistic and meditative but still enjoyable about it. Start by gathering some combination of the following:

Calcite	Tiger's-eye	Smoky quartz
Citrine	Rose quartz	Obsidian
Clear quartz	Malachite	Lapis lazuli
Jade	Green aventurine	Amethyst
Opal	Hematite	

The more crystals you have on hand, the bigger your grid will be, but it doesn't *have* to be big—a smaller grid will be just as powerful, and you can also intersperse the following herbs and flowers:

Sunflower	Crocuses	Parsley
Lavender	Evening primrose	Apple peel
Cinnamon sticks	Cardamom pods	Hazel
Lime or lemon peel	Basil	Vervain

Make sure that you have a total of some multiple of three (magic really likes the number three), and at least eighteen crystals and/or herbs. Now arrange your crystals and herbs by sight and feel. The goal is to create a balanced grid, so vary the dark and light colors of your crystals, rather than grouping them all together, and vary textures and shapes, so if you have some that are wand-shaped rather than rounded, place them in opposition to each other. Intersperse the herbs and flowers the same way, alternating with crystals and keeping them in a nice, balanced, geometric form. Make it pretty!

When your grid is complete, take a moment to activate it. Starting from the outside and working your way in toward the center, take a selenium or clear quartz wand, or even your finger, and draw lines connecting each crystal, bringing them into alignment with each other. Leave the grid in place for at least twenty-four hours.

MANIFESTATION SPELL
FOR A FRIEND'S DEEPEST DESIRE

You could definitely perform this spell on your own behalf, but our wishes for ourselves are sometimes clouded by our own doubts or our own desires. But a spell performed for someone else's benefit is incredibly pure and therefore more powerful.

Write down your friend's wish, whether it's to get into a certain school, go on a trip, perfect a new skill—whatever it may be. Fold the paper in half twice. Then take it outside and find a patch of clover. Carefully, lift the clover aside with its roots intact and place your paper beneath it. Pat the clover back in place and water it.

Over the next three days, visit your patch of clover. Stroke it, sing to it, and imagine your friend's wish being granted. Put all that imagining into the clover, so that it is receiving your intention from above and from below.

INTERLOCKING GRIMOIRES

As you and your friends have been working through your spells together, make sure you are writing down how they go, any tweaks or adjustments you've made, and any spells you've come up with on your own! You should each be keeping your own grimoires, your own books of magic.

In working all this magic together, you and your friends have formed a kind of coven. Now that's another loaded word—like witch, it feels like something scary. But it is nothing more than a group of like-minded, magical people—and you and your friends definitely count! A fun way to celebrate your coven is to link your grimoires.

Get the coven together, and have everyone open to a blank page deep in the grimoire. Arrange your books so that edges and corners are touching. Now, sketch a design to represent your coven. Include herbs you've found effective or crystals you've used, but also include something that represents each of you—choose an animal, an object or a symbol that really feels right. This is a collaborative project, so discuss! And then transfer your design to the center of your arranged books, so that it flows from one book to the other, joining them together.

FULFILLMENT

It's possible you're not familiar with this word, but it's an important one to know.

FUL-FILL-MENT. *1. Satisfaction or happiness as a result of achieving something one desires. 2. Satisfaction or happiness as a result of fully developing one's abilities or character.*

Let's look at both definitions. With the first one, we may often think about work/school—about getting good grades or struggling through homework. Being successful in school *is* satisfying, and it can lead to a happy, productive adult life. Working hard is important.

And yet, that's not all there is to it. The second definition talks about working on ourselves, for ourselves—not for any specific life goal. Exploring concepts that spark our interest, learning new skills, and developing our talents are also hard work, and they also lead to happiness and satisfaction with your life—and, perhaps more important, with yourself.

This section will help you navigate both definitions, providing you with the inner strength to manage the inevitable ups and downs, the courage to try something new, as well as the creativity and insight to figure out what truly makes you happy.

Creating

SPELL TO INVITE CREATIVITY

• • ● • •

For thousands of years, the moon has served as a symbol of mystery, of femininity, and of creativity. Her light can help us connect to our intuition and our creative energies. If you're looking to start a new project, make something, explore your artistic side, or even just be a little more imaginative, the moon can help you on your way.

She is at her most powerful on the full moon, of course, so plan in advance and try to work your spell on that night. Choose a crystal-like opal, garnet, or carnelian for creativity and also amazonite, lapis lazuli, or smoky quartz for intuition, since you will need both. Prepare an essential oil blend that includes a combination of jasmine, sandalwood, lavender, frankincense, or myrrh.

Sit so that the light of the moon falls upon your hands. You can do this just by being by a window. Choose your first crystal, and anoint it with essential oil by taking the tip of your finger and rubbing a drop of oil into the crystal. As you do, chant:

> *Let me see what is unseen*
> *Let my intuition be my guiding light*
> *Let me create, let me envision, let me imagine*
> *Let me be inspired, on this moonlit night*

Repeat with both of your crystals, and then let them bathe in the moonlight overnight. On the next night, tuck them under your pillow so that the mysteries they have received from the moon can be shown to you in your dreams.

SPELL TO INVITE SUCCESS

•• ● •• •

Remember those runes on page 7? Well, they're good for more than just writing in code—they can also help you work some powerful magic. Each of them has a specific meaning, and when they're linked together, they can grow ever more powerful.

Start by thinking about what success means to you and what kind of success you're looking for. Remember that success/fulfillment isn't just about academics, but about feeling valuable, doing good in the world, and, most importantly, simply being happy!

Give some thought to what exactly it is that you want to invite into your life, and then consider how to apply that to the runes. For example, if you want to pass a test, you might want to choose Isa and Mannaz, and combine them like so:

Or if you're trying to create something, like a piece of art or you're building or crafting something, you might combine Sowilo and Kenaz:

Or if you've got a big game coming up, you might choose Uruz and Ehwaz:

Once you have designed your rune combination, you now have to design your spell! You're an experienced witch now, so it's time to play with various spell forms and see what will work best for your needs.

For a test, you may want to sketch your rune on each of your study sheets, on your homework, anywhere that seems right. Mind you, this isn't a substitute for studying! You'll definitely still need to put the time and effort in, but your rune will help all your studying sink in. Then, the night before the test, after you've studied, sketch your rune one last time on a separate sheet of paper, and then bury it in the earth. You've prepared all you can, and you've done your best. It's time to let it go and see what happens.

For a craft, be creative! Can you add the rune to your design? If not (or if it would ruin the aesthetic), pause your project for a moment, and take time to create your rune. If you're working on a painting, paint the rune first, and hang it over your work as inspiration.

For sports, paint your rune on your water bottle, or if you can, sketch it on a tiny piece of paper and keep it in your pocket, so that it's there with you the whole time.

These are all just ideas to get you started. You know best how to achieve the success you want.

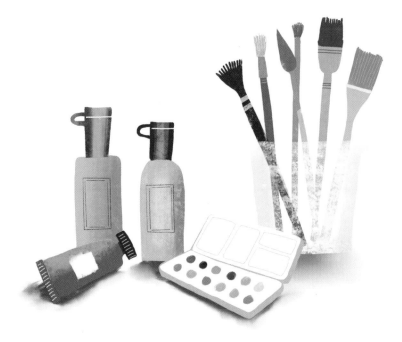

SIGIL MAGIC

Sigil magic is a lot like rune magic, in that it relies on symbols and meanings—but the difference is that *we* are the ones who create those symbols and imbue them with the meaning of our choice. It's fun, creative, and can be quite beautiful.

You design a sigil by writing out a short spell that speaks to what you want. So, for instance: Let All My Dreams Come True. Next, take out all but the first letters in each of the main words, so: LAMDCT. And here's when you get to be artistic about it! Take out a paper and pencil and create a beautiful image that incorporates

those letters but also—and this important!—renders them completely unrecognizable. You'll want to turn them sideways, add
embellishments, reverse them—anything that makes it so that,
unless you knew what they were, you wouldn't be able to see them.

You can use colored pencils, watercolors—whatever feels best
for you. Add crosses, arrows, swoops—you want to obscure the
meaning *and* make it beautiful.

Now comes the tricky part. You need to forget exactly what it
was you were trying to say. Sigil magic is different from other forms
of magic, because it requires a witch to *lose* her focus, rather than
maintain it. In this case, the spell works best without the influence
of the witch herself.

In order to do that, put the sigil away for a while. A full lunar cycle (the journey from one full moon to the next—basically a month) is a good length of time. At the end of that time, pull it out again. No worries if you still remember what you were trying to say—you'll forget eventually. Bring the sigil out, and then here's where the magic comes in: you need to distract yourself from it, so you're not thinking about it at all! And then, you take it a step further, so that you're not thinking about *anything*.

You know best how to achieve this. What makes you feel the most mindless, the most free of any thoughts or desires? Is it playing video games? Is it dancing? Is it running down a hill as fast as you can? Being completely goofy with your friends? Do whatever it is you need to do to feel completely relaxed, at ease, and free of worry or thought.

Once you've got that feeling, take a look at your sigil. Don't worry about trying to remember what it meant—stay relaxed, and just look at it. Let your mindless state be a reflection for it so that it can take what it needs from you.

And now you can do what you like with it! If you think it's pretty, hang it up! You can shove it in a drawer, paste it into your grimoire, burn it, anything—because whatever you do won't matter; it is already working its magic for you.

GRIS-GRIS FOR LUCK

• • • • • •

Luck magic can be tricky. If you think about luck in the traditional sense, then it's something that comes from outside us, like a leprechaun or the Roman goddess Fortuna or something—and often, there's a price to be paid for that good luck. However, if we remember that we are the creators of our own lives, then we know that there's a never-ending resource of positive energy. We can call it any number of things—including, on occasion, luck.

So how do we invite that positive energy, using the traditions and associations we have with luck? There are so many ways, but one of the easiest and most tangible is to create a gris-gris that you can carry around with you, to remind you that you always have access to your luck.

Start by picking the fabric for your bag. Red is considered lucky in several cultures, as are green and gold. But magic is always personal! What color makes you feel *good*, positive, and powerful? And remember, you can use any kind of cloth you like for a gris-gris! Do you have a favorite T-shirt that is maybe a bit too stained or too small to wear, but is still beloved? You can cut out a square and use that!

You really only need a four- or six-inch square, so work with what's handy. At the center of the square, place some combination of the following items:

Carnelian	Tiger's-eye	Clove
Aventurine	Irish moss	Basil
Jade	Poppy seeds	

Finally, take a penny, as pennies have a long tradition of holding good luck. Hold it in the palm of your hand and let it warm to the temperature of your skin. Bring your palm to your lips and whisper "A penny for luck!" so that your breath blows over the penny. Place it onto your gris-gris cloth and use a ribbon or a bit of string to pull it tight.

Keep your gris-gris with you whenever you feel like you need just a little bit of lucky energy.

Healing

SELF-LOVE RITUAL FOR WHEN
YOU DON'T GET IT RIGHT THE FIRST TIME

• • •• • •

Fulfillment will never be achieved without some failure along the way. If it were easy, it wouldn't be all that fulfilling, would it? Failure is an integral part of the process of reaching satisfaction and happiness.

That doesn't mean it's a pleasant experience. Whenever we fail at something—and particularly when it's something we really want to be good at—it *hurts*. We feel all kinds of emotions, and may decide that this failure along our journey means that we're not good at this, that we're never going to be good at this, and, sometimes, that's there's something wrong with *us* because we weren't successful this time.

Sometimes it helps to take a step back and reassess things. Imagine the person in this situation isn't *you*, but your best friend. You *know* this is just a minor setback. You *know* she's got this, and that if she were to give up now, you'd remind her to not give up.

We are often much more generous with others than we are with ourselves. This ritual will help you apply the same loving support, comfort, and encouragement to yourself that is so easy to give to others.

Start by treating yourself. You've had a hard day! Give yourself a little gift to make it better. Watch your favorite movie. Read a book. Get some fresh air. Blow off a little steam. Go shopping. Don't think about the failure, don't stew over it, and don't even think about how you'll do better next time—that's for later. Do something that feels *really good* for now.

Then, when you feel a bit lighter, gather some clear quartz, some lemon or lime essential oil, and a candle. Anoint the candle with your essential oil and light it. Hold your crystal in your palm.

Now you can allow yourself to think about your failure. Ask yourself what you could have done differently. The question is not about blame or about listing all the ways you screwed up; instead it's literal information-gathering. You can't fix what went wrong unless you *know* what went wrong.

Offer yourself the comfort you would give your best friend. You know what you would say, and you know what you need to hear. You can be just as kind to yourself as you would be to a friend.

Take hold of your clear quartz, and imagine next time—because you know there will be a next time! Imagine how *awesome* you'll do next time, and let your clear quartz absorb that image. And then, add in the possibility that it won't be perfect then, either! New problems might come up, problems that you're not able to antici-pate right now. Let yourself know in advance that if that happens, it's okay. It's just another step forward.

When you've filled your clear quartz with everything you need, blow out the candle. Let this failure go. It's done. Tuck the clear quartz somewhere for safekeeping, so that it will be there to sup-port you on your next try.

MINDFULNESS MEDITATION

• • ● • • •

You've probably heard the word *mindfulness* a lot, maybe even in school. It may sound a bit contradictory because you're actually trying to be *less* mindful, in a way. You're trying to get out of your own head and out of the tangled, circular thought patterns we can get into. You know how sometimes you just keep thinking the same thing, over and over, worrying and stressing over the same issue, even though you know obsessing about it won't do you any good?

Mindfulness can help with that. It's a practice of becoming aware of what's going on with you right this second, right now. You're not worrying about yesterday or tomorrow or even ten minutes from now—you are only focused on the present moment.

Of course, that sounds easy enough, but telling yourself to stop worrying is about as effective as telling a toddler not to want another lollipop. It just doesn't work that way. A mindfulness meditation practice offers a technique to help you get there—and it is something you *practice*. You can't expect yourself to "get it right," because, honestly, it isn't something that you can possibly do perfectly—so let go of that expectation right now. A mindfulness meditation is just a way of releasing and relieving stress.

Start by finding someplace quiet and comfortable. You don't have to move your body into a pretzel to meditate—you can do it sitting in a chair or lying on the floor or on your bed. Go ahead and get comfortable, just make sure you're not likely to fall asleep.

If your eyes want to close, go ahead and let them, but don't force it. If they'd rather stay open, just soften your gaze a bit by letting your vision blur and lowering your lashes about halfway.

Next, start to pay attention to your breathing. Just the act of noticing your breathing will change it. You'll find that you breathe more slowly, more deeply. Follow that breath. Pay attention to how it feels moving in and out of your body, as your chest rises and falls.

Your mind will start to wander. That's what minds do. When it does, don't get frustrated—that's just your brain doing its job. Gently remind it that it doesn't need to work so hard right now, and bring your focus back to your breath. You'll likely need to do this over and over again. That repetition is the core of a mindfulness meditation practice.

When you feel done—and how long you do this is entirely up to you—allow your eyes to open or become more alert. Allow yourself to feel your body in space, as it touches the floor or the chair. Feel the air in the room—is it warm? Is there a breeze? Notice any sounds you might hear, of neighbors or dogs barking or family members moving around, going about their day. Come back to the world.

BALM AGAINST DISAPPOINTMENT

Sometimes things don't work out, and sometimes there is nothing we could have done differently that would have produced a different result. Disappointment is an inevitable part of life, and it's not really one of those emotions where you can try to find the bright side. When you're feeling it, there is no bright side. When you're in the midst of disappointment, there isn't any way to make it go away.

You can ease it, though. You can take care of yourself, and allow yourself to feel all that you're feeling, without adding judgment or anger and making it worse than it is. This balm, a form of herb-witchery, can help hold off any of those related emotions that only make things harder. You'll want to prepare this balm now, so that you have it on hand for whenever you might need it.

Start by creating an herbal oil. Collect some combination of lemon balm, marjoram, basil, rose, and lavender. If they're dried, bruise them a bit by crushing them between your fingertips, and if they're fresh, chop them up a little bit to release their juices. Place them in a small jar, and cover them entirely with oil. Use a mild carrier oil like almond or olive oil, something gentle and soothing for your skin. Allow your jar to sit in the sunshine for six weeks or so.

When your herbal oil is ready, pour out a quarter cup of it. Heat it in a small saucepan over low heat and add a quarter ounce of beeswax. When the beeswax has melted, remove the pan from the heat. Pour your mixture into a clean jar or container and stir in thirty drops total of a combination of rose, lavender, angelica, and chamomile essential oils. Cover the jar and let it rest for at least two hours.

When you need it, smooth the balm on your hands, your heart, and the soles of your feet. It will comfort you.

STORYTELLING MAGIC

• • • • • •

Storytelling is some of the most powerful magic there is. Think about myths, legends, fairy tales, and the way they have shaped various cultures around the world. They are our way of connecting with the earth, of making sense of seemingly senseless things, and of explaining what it is to be a human being.

Stories can have an impact on a grand scale like that, but also on a smaller scale. The stories we tell ourselves are how we make sense of our own experience. It is how we understand who we are. And we tell ourselves these stories all day, every day, without even realizing it.

Think about a time when you tried something new. You were

nervous, and you didn't get it exactly right. Maybe you were onstage and you forgot your lines, or you were skateboarding and you got hurt. Whatever it was, it didn't end well.

Those are the facts of the situation. The story part came in when you tried to explain it to yourself. The story you told was that you're not good at public speaking, that you're shy, and that you should never, ever put yourself in a situation like that again. Or it was that you're uncoordinated, scared, and not meant to be standing on something that isn't solid ground.

All of that is just a story. The facts are that you forgot your lines, that you fell. Everything else is just something you made up, and it is no more real than a fairy tale. You have absolutely no evidence that forgetting your lines one time means that you're not good at this, and falling is something every single skateboarder has experienced (the same is true for being onstage, honestly).

But we have a tendency to tell ourselves stories that say *we can't* or *we shouldn't* or *we're not good at this*. And we do it not because we don't love ourselves enough, but because we want to protect ourselves. Screwing up feels terrible! Falling down is painful! We want to avoid these things at all costs, and so without thinking about it, we tell ourselves stories that will stop us from putting ourselves in these situations again.

But you have to ask yourself what you really want. Think back to before you screwed up, before you fell. Were you excited? Did you want to succeed at it?

You know perfectly well that in order to really succeed at anything, you have to deal with some failures along the way, and if you tell yourself a story that says the failure is all there is, you'll never get past it.

Now, most of us can't stop that kind of storytelling right away. It's a natural tendency, and when we're in the moment of failure, our protective instincts are going to kick in. That's okay. Take some time to feel that disappointment, and maybe take comfort in the balm on page 46.

But when you're ready, pull out your grimoire and write yourself a new story. Start from the beginning. You can have fun with this—you can go full fairy tale and turn the skateboard into a dragon that you must learn to ride. You can be yourself, or you can be a pixie with wings and flower petals. When you get to the moment of failure, write that failure. The pixie fell off the dragon into a fiery pit. Write how the pixie burned.

But then, let her rise from the ashes. Let the fire have given her the strength to master the dragon, though she knew it would take lots of hard work and probably a lot more falls. Keep writing until she is soaring through the skies.

And then, with this new story in your heart, get back out there and try again.

SPELL TO INVITE SLEEP

••●••

From time to time, we all have trouble sleeping. It can happen when we're stressed, when we're worried, when we're distracted. And "trouble sleeping" can mean many different things—it can include nightmares, trouble falling asleep, trouble staying asleep, trouble feeling calm, and trouble letting go of the day.

In order to cast an effective spell, you need to know exactly what it is you're addressing. What's been keeping you up?

- **NIGHTMARES.** You'll need garnet and chamomile.

- **TROUBLE LETTING GO OF THE DAY.** You'll need selenite and yarrow.

- **ANXIETY.** You'll need hematite and lavender.

- **TROUBLE FALLING ASLEEP.** You'll need lepidolite and vervain.

- **TROUBLE STAYING ASLEEP.** You'll need celestite and vervain.

- **JUST DON'T WANT TO GO TO SLEEP.** You'll need amethyst and lavender.

About half an hour or so before bed, start your spell by brewing a cup of tea, using your herb of choice. Add a little milk and honey to make it extra soothing and sweet. As you sip your tea, hold your crystal in your palm. Roll it around between your fingers, and allow it to accept whatever it is that's been keeping you awake. If you've got something specific, like anxiety about an upcoming test or a fight you've just had, give it to the crystal. But it's also fine if you're not quite sure what it is, but *something* has been keeping you up. The crystal will figure it out and absorb it.

Then, allow the crystal to transfer its healing energies to you. Take what it has to offer.

When you've finished your tea, get ready for bed. Make sure your bedspread is turned down and your pillows are arranged just how you like them. Make sure the lights are low and your room is quiet (earplugs are handy for this if other people are still awake and noisy in your house). And, of course, turn off any screens and silence any phones.

Climb into bed, but don't lie down yet. Sit cross-legged, with your palms open, your crystal resting in your nondominant hand. Sit there for a few minutes, imagining that sense of heaviness you feel when you wake up in the morning, when you're tired and just want a few more minutes' sleep. Feel it now. Imagine a dream you want to have. Imagine putting all your worries in a little box and setting them aside for now. They'll be there waiting when you wake up in the morning—you don't need them now.

Did your mom ever sing you to sleep? Some lullaby you remember from when you were really small? That's some powerful magic right there. She probably would be delighted to sing it to you again, or if you want, you can sing to yourself, softly—no one can hear you. And if not, simply whisper:

> *I am safe while I sleep*
> *My rest is deep*
> *My worries, they will keep*
> *While I am fast asleep*

Place your crystal under your pillow. If your eyes are ready to close, allow them to do so. Otherwise, keep the lights low and read a beautiful (but maybe not terribly exciting) book. Let sleep come when it will.

Empowering

CONCENTRATION POTION

● ● ●● ● ●

We all get distracted sometimes. It's impossible not to. We can blame the internet, phones, television, texting, but in all likelihood, people have been easily distracted since well before that, just by different things (birds and books, maybe?). It's an eternal struggle.

The quickest and easiest method for improving concentration is to brew yourself a cup of tea.

Tea may not sound like your idea of a potion, but that's all a potion is—a mixture of magical ingredients, added to water that you can then drink. There's nothing saying a potion has to be lumpy and disgusting. In fact, it can be delicious!

For a full pot of tea, you'll want a tablespoon's worth of the following dried herbs. For just a cup, you'll only need a teaspoon. Blend together a mixture of:

• ROSEMARY, for memory

• MINT, for finding flow

• SAGE, for wisdom

• CINNAMON STICK, to enhance brain activity

Put it in a tea strainer, then let your tea steep for around ten minutes. (If you're brewing just a mug, cover it so it doesn't get cold.) While it's steeping, surround it with amethyst, lapis lazuli, and smoky quartz, and when it's done, stir in honey and a squeeze of lemon.

CRYSTAL GRID FOR THE NIGHT
BEFORE A TEST

• • ● • • •

Unlike the crystal grid on page 25, this grid is very specific: it's about focus. You'll want to include some of the following:

- Fluorite, to keep you motivated as you study
- Clear quartz, to help you remember everything
- Aquamarine, to help you feel less nervous
- Citrine, to give you confidence
- Jade, to keep you working hard
- Hematite, to keep you from getting distracted

You'll want at least nine crystals total, and be sure to use a multiple of three if you have more than nine. For this grid, you're going to create a big swirl. First, arrange your crystals in order. You can group them by size, by color, by shape, by function—do whatever feels right, but make sure you're organizing them somehow. This will help your mind remember to organize all the information you're cramming into it.

Once you've determined the order of your crystals, start at the center of your swirl and build it out, round and round. Once it's complete, activate your grid with your selenium or quartz point by dragging it through the labyrinth, along the path you've created, starting at the center and working your way out. Leave your grid next to you as you study.

DIY ORACLE DECK

• • ● • • •

An oracle deck is simply a set of cards with images on them. If you buy them at the store, they'll come with a little booklet explaining what each card means, or they'll have the meanings written on the back. They can be used for inspiration, if you're trying to decide how to start a project. They can offer advice for a tricky situation or help you figure out what it is you really want.

Like most things involving magic, the most powerful deck is one you've created yourself. It will be personal to you, and so the meanings you give the various images will signify more to you than they could to anyone else—and therefore will speak to you more clearly.

Your deck can be as large or small as you want, and you can keep adding to it over time. You'll want to start with at least thirty cards. Use some nice, firm card stock and cut it into a shape that feels right to you—it can be rectangular, square, circular, triangular, anything!

Next, choose a medium. Do you like to draw? Are you into collage? Do you like to paint? Get your supplies together. You may also want some Mod Podge or other protective covering, so your cards don't wear out too quickly.

When you're ready to start designing your cards, consider the following ideas:

• Characters from books or movies

• Animals

• Mythical creatures

• Places in the world you'd like to visit

- Historical figures you admire

- Music

- Lines of poetry

- Scenes from nature

- Herbs or flowers

These are all just suggestions to help you get the creative juices flowing—remember, you know best what will work for you!

Once you've created your deck, spend a little time with it. Hold each card, and give it some thought—what does it inspire in you? You can jot down your meanings in your grimoire, though you'll find you need to update it as they will shift and deepen the more you use the cards.

When your deck is ready, you can perform your first reading! There are several ways to do this. If your question is simple, or if you don't even have a question and just want some general guidance, you can simply shuffle the cards. Keep going until one of them sticks out or falls out—that card is volunteering to answer your question. It's up to you, though, to interpret what it's trying to say.

If you're dealing with a more complex issue that can't be answered by just one card, you can do a three-card reading by shuffling your cards and spreading them out in front of you. Choose one card and lay it faceup—this card represents the past. Your second card represents the present, and your third card represents the future.

SPELL FOR COURAGE

• • ● • •

We do things that scare us every day. We talk to people we don't know very well, we try new things, we perform in public, we take risks. Most of the time, we don't even think about it—being brave is just a part of life. But sometimes we are required to be *extra* brave, and in those cases, we can use a little extra magic.

You will need the following supplies:

• Selenium or clear quartz wand

• A combination of myrrh, ginger and frankincense essential oils

• A candle

Sit cross-legged on the ground or floor and use your wand to draw a sacred circle around yourself and your supplies. Anoint your candle with your essential oils and light it. Once the flame has grown tall and still, prepare to anoint your wrists. Recite the following incantation as you do so:

In my hands, I carry strength.

As you anoint the soles of your feet, say:

I walk with determination

As you anoint the base of your throat, say:

I speak without fear

And as you anoint your temples, say:

My mind, my thoughts and my soul
are the source of my power.
Let me have the courage to hold all
that I must carry
To journey wherever life takes me
To speak what is true and right
And to know, always, that everything I need,
I already have within me.

FAMILY

In so many ways, our families are the most important people in our lives. We see them every day, we live with them, eat with them, and no matter what, they will always be there, forever. Unlike with our friends, we don't get to *choose* them—this is the family we have, and for better or worse, we're stuck with them.

They can drive us crazy. Nobody can irritate you more or find ways to hit where you're most sensitive, than your parents or siblings. And at the same time, no one can make you feel more loved, can make you feel like you're seen for who you truly are, than your family. They know us better than anyone else can, because they have seen every part of us. They *are* a part of us.

This kind of connection is so powerful and so challenging because it goes both ways. We can hurt and support the members of our family in all the same ways they can hurt and support us. In fact, these relationships are the ones most under our control. That golden rule about treating others as you wish to be treated? It works most of the time but is never more effective than when dealing with your family. Do you wish that your mom would assume the best of you? If you assume the best of her, you'll find that she responds in kind. Do you wish that your older brother would include you more? Share with him some of the interesting things you're doing, and as he realizes he actually enjoys your company, he'll spend less time ignoring you.

But it doesn't *always* work, and it certainly isn't easy. This section will provide you with some spells, tools, and practices that will help you enjoy the good times and navigate your way through the more stressful times.

Creating

SPELL TO INVITE PEACE IN CHAOS

Home is supposed to be the place where you feel calmest, safest, and most relaxed. And often it is! But sometimes, in the rush of various energies, needs, anxieties, and demands, it can get kind of stressful. There isn't really any preventing this, but you can lessen the effect it has on you.

Start by creating a gris-gris bag. In this case, use a very soft cloth, maybe lavender or blue in color, shades that enhance feelings of peace and calm. Make it a little bigger than usual, maybe a five-inch square this time. Fill it with dried lavender, and add basil, violet, chamomile, or lemon balm if you like. Find a small item that represents each member of your family, including yourself: it could be a solitary earring of your sister's (say if she's lost the other one), a guitar pick of your father's, or a piece of paper with a quote from one of your mother's favorite authors. Gather them all together into your gris-gris.

To activate your gris-gris, surround it with turquoise, hematite, and rose quartz. Meditate over it for a few minutes, thinking about peaceful moments with your family—be as specific as you can, because you want to infuse your gris-gris with that energy. Lift your gris-gris to your heart and bow your head.

Keep your gris-gris in a room where you and your family spend a lot of time together—*and* a room where arguments or other stresses often happen. If there's a mad rush to get out the door in the morning, and everyone is bumping into each other in the kitchen, then maybe tuck it into the back of a cupboard. If you share a room with your sister, then you might consider tucking it away in part of your shared space.

But don't lose track of where you put it! In moments where everything is chaotic and stressful, fetch it out and hold it to your heart. Breathe for just a few moments—even if you're in a rush, it's worth it.

From time to time you may need to reactivate your gris-gris. Just repeat the ritual, surrounding it with crystals and meditating over it as you infuse it with the positive, peaceful energy of your family.

BINDING SPELL TO BRING
EACH OTHER CLOSER

• • ● ● • •

Sometimes we can feel really distant from those we love, even when they're right there. We can go about our days together and not really *see* each other as we move through the routines of morning rush-school-homework-dinner-bed. We can feel lonely even when we're surrounded by people who love us.

When this happens, try casting a gentle binding spell to help you feel that closeness again. Collect a few strands of your own hair and combine them with some hairs of the person—or persons!—you want to feel closer to. Hold them in your hands, and then tie them together in a knot.

Take the knot of hair outside, and bury it in the earth, where it can regenerate, change, and help create new life. As you do so, remember that you are bound by DNA, by love, by living together day after day and that nothing can ever break that connection.

And then, having been empowered by this spell, start being the change you want to see. Instead of watching television, go hang out with your sister. Help with dinner. Suggest a family game night. You have more impact than you know and can make your family dynamic into exactly what you want it to be.

FAMILY HERALDRY

•••••••

In the 1100s, knights finally got smart enough to wear helmets to protect their faces in battle . . . but then, nobody knew who they were fighting. And so began the tradition of heraldry—it's a picture, a symbol, to proclaim who you are. It is how we represent ourselves to the world. Flags do the same thing. Stars and Stripes? Everyone knows what that means. And a flag is also a reminder of what we want to *be* in the world—whether that is brave, loyal, mighty, or generous.

Creating your own family heraldry is a fun project to do with your parents and siblings, if they're up for it, and it will help you all be more conscious about what kind of family you want to be to the outside world and more importantly, to each other. Draw it out in your grimoire, and then create a larger one that you can hang by your door!

Start by choosing a base color or colors:

- GOLD, or *Or* as it was known in the Middle Ages: generosity
- SILVER/WHITE or *Argent*: peace
- PURPLE or *purpure*: justice
- RED or *gules*: strength
- BLUE or *azure*: loyalty
- GREEN or *vert*: hope
- BLACK or *sable*: constancy
- ORANGE or *tenne*: striving

Next, you can choose an animal to represent your family:

- **LION:** bravery

- **EAGLE:** power and nobility

- **BEAR:** strength

- **BUTTERFLY:** transformation

- **CROW:** ingenuity

- **DOG:** loyalty

- **FOX:** trickery

- **OWL:** wisdom and insight

Or you can use mythical creatures:

- **PHOENIX:** rebirth

- **CENTAUR:** healing, instinct

- **MERMAID:** creativity, mystery

- **DRAGON:** protection, wisdom

- **UNICORN:** purity, magic

- **GRIFFIN:** watchfulness, courage

You can embellish with the following lines:

- **NEBULY:** clouds, air

- **WAVY:** ocean, water

- **EMBATTLED:** protection

- **ENGRAILED:** earth, land

- **INDENTED:** fire

SWEETENING SPELL

• • ● ● • •

Sweetening spells have their roots in the voodoo traditions of New Orleans, and they're some of the most positive magic there is. They are used to "sweeten" a situation or relationship. If you've been fighting a lot with a sibling or parent, or just generally feel like you're butting heads all the time, this spell can help take out any bitterness you may be feeling and rediscover the love you have for each other.

Take a piece of paper and write the name of the person you're struggling with three times. Then rotate the paper ninety degrees and write your own name three times, so that it crosses over. It will look like the letters are weaving together. Draw a circle around your interlocking names. Following the line of circle, write what you want in the relationship. You could write:

- Laughter
- Joy
- Love
- Fun
- Support
- Trust

Or write down any combination of the above. But—and this is both important and kind of fun—you must write in a continuous line. If you feel comfortable with cursive, do use it, but if not, just print letters without picking up your pencil or pen so that these are in a continuous line. So laughter over and over might look like the illustration on the opposite page.

Continue until the circle is complete.

When you're finished, fold the paper in half, and in half again and again until it's nice and small. Take a small jar of honey, dip in a teaspoon, and make room for your piece of paper—remember, part of sweetening a relationship will include sweetening yourself, so take a taste. Then dip your folded paper into the jar and seal it up tight.

FAMILIARS

•••••

The idea of a witch having a familiar is as common as a witch having a broom—it's just what we do! But a witch's familiar doesn't necessarily have to be a black cat. It can be any creature at all—a deer, a dog, a dragonfly, anything. The word *familiar* means "intimate, very friendly, on a family footing, of the household," so what makes a creature your familiar is your relationship, since familiars are more than just pets. They are family and there to support you and the magic you work in the world.

There are many ways to find your familiar, but most often he or she will approach you. Often, a wild creature will choose us, as when the same deer comes around all the time, or a blue jay pecks from your hand. Or your familiar may have found its way to you through an adoption shelter or a pet store.

If you think an animal is your familiar, but you aren't quite sure, you must ask it. For a pet, get as close as you can and stroke or snuggle your pet in a way you know it enjoys.

For a wild creature, physical contact may not be an option. In that case, simply get as close as the animal will comfortably allow, and ask silently: *Are you my familiar? Would you like to be?* Listen for the answer.

If it is a yes, you must make an offering to consecrate the relationship, to honor this choice. Favorite treats, a new bed, or even just time spent at a favorite activity works for a pet. For a wild creature, make an offering that feels right. Some might accept food you leave out, but others are too naturally cautious of humans, however connected they may feel with you. If food won't work, leave an offering of crocuses, evening primrose, mint, parsley, or yarrow, to symbolize your connection.

Healing

MEDITATION: KEEP CALM AND
LOOK FOR THE GOOD

••••••

Meditation is one of a witch's most valuable tools, but the problem with it is that it's really more preventive magic or magic for recovery, rather than magic that works in the moment. If you meditate regularly, you'll be less prone to anxiety, anger, and other painful emotions, and meditation can help heal from those emotions when you have the time and space to do so.

But when you're in the midst of a stressful situation, you can't exactly close your eyes and meditate it away—or at least, not in the traditional sense.

This meditation practice does not require a quiet room and the ability to concentrate. You don't have to sit or close your eyes or anything like that. Instead, this is an active, waking meditation that can be done even in the middle of an argument, sitting on the sidelines while someone else is fighting, or just in the general anxiety of living with people we love.

All you need to do is to put your attention on five things that are outside of the stressful moment.

Say you're standing in line at the grocery store, and your mom is really stressed out about something. It doesn't really have to do with you, but she's upset and so she's snapping at you. Understandably, this makes you angry. Before you snap back at her, take a moment to notice five things—and they can be anything at all. Something you hear, something you smell, something you see or feel.

• A song you like is playing.

• The basil you're buying smells really good.

• The tomatoes are really an astonishingly beautiful red.

• The lady ahead of you in line is buying a birthday cake.

• Your mom put your favorite snack in the cart for you.

Just the act of paying attention to something else, to something every day and normal but also positive, can change how you feel.

Maybe now, instead of snapping at your mom (which would be understandable, but wouldn't make the situation better), you can give her a minute and then eventually, calmly, let her know that she's upsetting you, though you know she doesn't mean to.

HOME CLEANSING SPELL

We pick up energy as we move through our day. Our interactions with others leave a mark, even if we don't realize it. If a friend is grouchy, we often absorb that emotion and bring it home with us, even though it isn't ours to carry. And this is true of everyone—your mother, your father, your siblings. Every member of your family brings home all the things they picked up throughout their day.

As often as not, this is a good thing! We bring joy, laughter, silliness, and inspiration home with us every day. But negative energies can hitch a ride, too, and when that happens, we need to know how to boot them out.

First, do a sweeping spell. It doesn't get more traditionally witchy than that! Sweep your doorstep and entryway, brushing everything out and away (if this earns you bonus points with your parents, so much the better).

Place selenite in the four corners of your house or as close to the corners as you can get. Leave them there overnight, and they will collect and break up any energy trapped in your house—but make sure to cleanse them afterward!

Finally, do a little smudging. Sage is traditional, but you could also use palo santo or incense. It's likely you'll want to check with your parents on this one, and maybe have them do it with you! Light your smudge stick or incense, blow it out so it is just smoldering, then carry it with you through your house, wafting its smoke up walls, against windows, and in corners. Make sure you have a bowl or shell handy to catch any ashes that may fall.

CLEANSING RITUAL

Sometimes the negative energies come from within the house, from your mom or your dad or your siblings, and clearing your home won't do the trick. This can happen. *Everybody* puts out negative energy from time to time—it's part of being human.

But that doesn't mean you have to keep carrying this energy. It's theirs, not yours, and they will deal with it in their own way, however they see fit. There's nothing you can do about that. What you can do is literally wash it away.

If you have a bathtub, great. If not, a simple sink or basin will do. Fill the tub or sink with warm, clear water. Add in some essential oils, including lavender, sage, lemon, or lime. You don't need much, just a few drops. Next, stir in some sea salt and let it dissolve. Just a tablespoon or two for a sink, and a cup for a bath.

Either immerse yourself in the bath, or splash the water on your face. The water will cleanse you, the oils will uplift you, and the salt will absorb any toxins. (Bonus: it's actually good for your skin!) Take your time here, if you want, using a washcloth to gently scrub or just relaxing and reading in the warm water. Let it all go.

FORGIVENESS SPELL

Our families can hurt our feelings more than anyone else can—but it goes both ways, so that *we* can do more harm to those who love us than we ever could to anyone else. We are not perfect, and so sometimes we hurt those we love the most. We can be thoughtless, or selfish, unintentionally cruel, or simply inconsiderate. Everyone does this, sometimes—again, we're human.

When this happens, we need to seek forgiveness. Because it is so easy to be hurt by those you love, it is often very difficult to forgive them. Your family needs your help with this, because of course they won't feel better until they forgive you. A grudge is a heavy burden.

Start by writing down what it is that you're seeking forgiveness for. Take your time and be honest. Don't write excuses or reasons for your behavior—just write the thing itself. But don't beat yourself up, either! There's no need for anger or blame here, even if it's against yourself (maybe especially if it's against yourself). Just be matter-of-fact.

When you've finished, light a candle, and make sure you have a plate nearby. Stare into the flame. Now is the time to think about the emotions—put yourself in the shoes of the person you hurt and imagine their feelings. Then think about the reasons behind your actions, whether it's the hard day you had, the fact that you'd been hurt, too, or just genuine thoughtlessness—that you didn't mean it. Be compassionate toward yourself. We can't ask for forgiveness from others until we're ready to receive it from ourselves first.

Take your piece of paper and hold it to the flame. Once it's caught fire, place it carefully on the plate, so that it burns safely. When it has burned down to ash, blow out the candle. Take the ashes and bury them, returning them to the earth.

You have now dissolved the energy of the hurt, but your spell can only get you part of the way to true forgiveness. If you haven't apologized already, do so now, coming from the place of compassion you reached when you put yourself on the other side of the hurt. And if the apology isn't enough, ask some questions. What would make this right? Is it just time? Are there amends to be made? Then listen.

Empowering

GUARDIAN FOR YOUR HOME

······

While we are the best source of our own power and magic, it can be useful to channel that energy into an object, so that it can protect and empower your home and family even when your attention is elsewhere. This object will act as a guardian for your home, watching over you and those you love, as you imbue it with the power of that love.

You can use anything you like! A toy, a crystal, a trinket—anything will do, though it's nice to use some kind of family heirloom or any kind of object that has some sort of meaning to your family. A vase that belonged to your grandmother, a shell you found together at the beach, a little figurine of an animal you all love—look around and see if you can find something that feels right.

Once you've settled on the object, the first step is to cleanse it. You can do this by surrounding it with crystals overnight—clear quartz or selenite are good choices—or by doing some smudging. Salt water will work, too, if the object won't be harmed in the process.

Then, set some intentions. What exactly do you want your guardian to do? Offer protection from negative energy? Prevent arguments, or at least soften them? Generally de-stress? Write it down in your grimoire and read it to your guardian. When you and your guardian are both clear on its job, take it for a walk around the house. It's not new here, but it has a new role and it should get to know the place it's protecting. If your family is into it, you can introduce them to their guardian.

Finally, settle on a good place for it, somewhere you will see it. It will need occasional encouragement, maybe some gratitude for its hard work. You can pet it, make occasional offerings, and from time to time you should cleanse it and reinvoke your intentions to keep your spell active.

ALL-ENCOMPASSING CRYSTAL GRID FOR HARMONY, PROTECTION, AND LOVE

• • • • • •

This grid will require you to get every member of your family on board, if not for the process of making it, then at least for its existence, because it's going to be *big*. The idea here is to cover your entire house, so that the energy of your grid permeates every inch of your space and every person who inhabits it.

Start by figuring out the focus of your grid. For something this big, it's okay to be a little general, like "love," "protection," or "harmony." Once you have your intention in place, gather every crystal you have. At minimum, you'll need one for each room in your house, but the more the merrier! Next, you'll want to program them; you'll likely be using some crystals whose primary purpose isn't exactly aligned with the focus of your grid, but that's not a problem! All you need to do is hold each crystal to your heart and focus on your intention. The crystal will align itself to meet your needs.

Begin your grid in the very center of your home. This might take a bit to figure out, but once you have it, place your first crystal on the floor, right in that spot. Work in a swirl from there, expanding away from the center of the room, going around your house, placing crystals as you go. You can start by being conservative, using only a few crystals, and then go back and add more crystals until you've incorporated each one.

When you're finished, it's time to activate it. Take your selenium or clear quartz wand and walk the path you've created through your house. Touch each and every crystal as you go, staying focused on your intention.

Once your grid has been activated, you'll probably only want to leave it up for an hour or so, partly because accidentally stepping on a crystal can really hurt! But not to worry—a spell this big and powerful doesn't need much time to work. When you're ready to take it down, gather your crystals in the opposite direction, so that you're working from the outside in toward the center of your home.

FAMILY LOVE SPELL

When you feel like you and your family are in a bit of a rut, that you're having a hard time communicating with each other, that everyone's stressed all the time and just kind of going through the motions of school-work-eat-sleep without really enjoying each other, try this spell.

If it's something your family wants to do with you, that's great, but they don't *need* to. As always, you have everything you need, all by yourself. For this spell, start by clearing all the negative energy that is present. Do some sage smudging, or even just meditate for a moment, concentrating on dissipating all of those messy, stressful feelings.

Then, as described on page 63, use your selenium wand to draw a sacred circle around you and anyone else that might be participating in the spell. If you're alone, sit cross-legged, with your palms open on your knees, but if you have someone with you, sit across from each other or in a circle and hold hands.

Take three deep, cleansing breaths together. Then list three things you love about each of the members of your family—and then list three things you know they love about you, too. If you're in a group, have everyone take turns doing this. If you're alone, place your hands on your heart and say, "I love you, I love you, I love you." If you're together with your family, squeeze each other's hands tight, and say it in a chorus, all together.

Finally—hug it out! If some or all of your family is there with you, get in on a big group hug. If you've done the spell alone, make time throughout the rest of the day to hug each member of your family, if you can. You don't have to give them a reason, just put all your love into your arms and your heart. For anyone who isn't around to give a hug to, hug yourself with your arms tight, and send them your hug energetically. They'll feel it, even if they don't know where it's coming from.

CELEBRATION RITUALS

• • ● • •

We celebrate with our families all the time—at birthdays, at holidays, around our achievements and our milestones. These kinds of celebrations are deeply important, but sometimes, as we get older, they change and become less than they once were. Maybe Christmas has become commercialized, maybe we would rather spend our birthdays with our friends, or maybe some kind of conflict always seems to arise around the holidays.

When this happens, it's important to find other rituals, other ways of celebrating with your family. You can create new and different holidays. Maybe you can celebrate anniversaries or make an effort to go camping together at the same place at the same time every year. Rituals and celebrations can happen for any reason, at any time.

Or, if you like, you can go further back in time, further even than Thanksgiving or Christmas, and take part in rituals and traditions that have held families together for thousands of years. The following are pagan holidays, scattered throughout the year and inspired by the equinoxes and solstices, as well as the yearly harvest. Our modern lives aren't nearly so bound to the seasons as they were when we each grew our own food, but an awareness of those seasons can help us feel connected to the earth, to what has come before, and to those with whom we share our lives.

- IMBOLC (IM-bullug). February 2. On this day, we celebrate the coming end of winter and begin to get to work. It's time to clean house, to set some intentions, and get ready to sow some good in the world. You and your family can celebrate by going for a walk in the woods, hunting for signs of spring. You can make a Brigid's Cross to honor the Irish goddess of fire and healing, and you can light candles throughout the house, to welcome the light back to the world.

- OSTARA (OH-star-ah). Spring Equinox. Closely linked with Easter, this day celebrates the midpoint of spring and the balance between night and day. By now, the leaves on the trees have budded, flowers have begun to bloom, and we can see the work we've done begin to blossom. Celebrate by working in a garden. If you don't have one, you can find a park to volunteer at or a neighborhood garden. There is always a way to get your fingers into the dirt.

- BELTANE (BAY-al-TIN-uh). May 1. The most joyful holiday of them all, Beltane is a celebration of life, of the pleasures of being alive in the world. You can celebrate by playing outside— maybe a game of Frisbee or soccer all together or just rolling around in the grass. It's warm enough to camp on Beltane in most places, and building a bonfire is a traditional way to enjoy the holiday.

- LITHA (LIE-tha). Summer Solstice, the traditional Midsummer Night's Eve. This a night when the veil between this world and the next is thin. On this shortest night of the year, we honor the sun and the forces for good in this world. If you can, get up with the dawn and watch the sun rise, celebrating the miracle we experience every day.

- LAMMAS (Luh-MAHS). August 1–2. This is the start of the harvest season. The heat of summer is coming to an end, and all the hard work we've put in over the course of the year finally comes to fruition. Lammas means "loaf-mass," and it describes an offering of loaves of bread to the Green Man (the god of nature) or the sun god. Baking a loaf of bread and offering it either to a representation of nature or even just sharing it with your family is a wonderful way to celebrate the work you have done together, in this eighth month of the year.

- **MABON** (MAY-bun). Fall Equinox. Mabon is a Welsh god of the harvest, but this second harvest of the year is less about bounty and more about reflection. As on Ostara, night and day are equal, and so the purpose of a Mabon celebration is to seek that balance, to become aware of both the darkness and the light within ourselves. This is a night spent in conversation, maybe telling stories together, playing music together, or just being with one another.

- **SAMHAIN** (Sow-in). October 31. You are definitely already celebrating Samhain every year! Trick-or-treating in costumes dates back to how people used to dress in white, or as opposite genders, in order to confuse any harmful spirits that might be lurking on this day that honors the relationship between life and death. It is a little spooky—but death is a part of life, and Samhain is a time to *enjoy* that spookiness and to reach out to those we love who have moved on.

- **YULE** (YEW-ell). December 21. On this the longest night of the year, we celebrate the end of winter. From here on out, the sun will rise sooner and stay with us longer, and we celebrate its life-giving warmth. Light a candle as the sun sets for its longest sleep, and make a wish for the coming year. What do you want to have? What do you want to leave behind?

CONCLUSION

I'm not going to say, "Congratulations, you're a witch now," because the truth is, you were a witch the whole time. You always had all of this power within you, and all of the magic that you have learned so far is just the very beginning. You've started herb magic, crystal magic, hearth magic, spellwork, candle magic, ritual magic, and lore from mystical practices throughout the world.

Now you can take what you've learned and make it your own. Your grimoire contains everything *you* have brought to this shared understanding of what magic is. Because here's the thing—there is no Dumbledore or Gandalf, no high wizard or mage who has more wisdom than you do. No one knows more than you do, as the most powerful magic is worked through using your own instincts and imagination.

Trust those instincts and embrace your own imagination and creativity. This is the true power, the true path to living a magical life.

Fly, little witch!

GLOSSARY

ALTAR. A place to honor your craft, by connecting with the earth, with your ancestors, and with those you admire. It can be small or large and filled with things that have meaning to you.

COVEN. The traditional name for a group of witches who often work together.

CRYSTAL GRID. The practice of laying out certain crystals in a geometric fashion, so that they work together to promote a specific purpose or intention.

DIVINATION. The art of seeing into the future or into something hidden.

GRIMOIRE. Also known as a Book of Shadows, this is a witch's reference guide, where she keeps notes on her spellwork.

GRIS-GRIS. A charm, usually a small bag, used as a physical representation of a spell.

HERALDRY. Traditional symbols used to help define who is who and what they represent.

HERB MAGIC. The practice of incorporating plants into your craft; a specialty of hearth or hedge witches. Often used for healing.

LUNAR CYCLE. The full transition of the moon through all its phases, from new moon to full and back again.

MAGIC CIRCLE. Certain spells require creating a sacred space, a circle to hold the power in place for the duration of the spell. You can do this by drawing an invisible circle around you with a selenite crystal, or you can create a physical circle with salt, crystals, herbs, stones, or flowers—whatever feels right for the spell!

MANIFESTATION. This has many definitions—in this case, it means the power to make something you want to have happen actually appear in your life.

RUNES. Ancient magic symbology, often used for divination.

SIGILS. A created symbol imbued with magical power.

ACKNOWLEDGMENTS

Thank you, Allison Cohen, for your vision and sense of fun and play—I have loved working with you. Thank you to Frances Soo Ping Chow for the gorgeous design, and to Hannah Jones for making it all work! Thank you Ashley Benning for keeping me honest and catching lo those many commas (I have a problem). Thank you also to Julie Matysik for making me a part of the RP Kids family, and to Valerie Howlett for getting Junior Witch out into the world.

Uta Krogmann, your illustrations have brought this book to vibrant life—they make my heart happy.

Thank you to Shannon Fabricant for getting this ball rolling— you keep me happy and busy, friend!

Thank you to Dave for, as always, putting up with all the crafting and rune-reading and crystals all over the place. Thank you to Mom and Dad, Hannah and Tulani for the eyeroll-free pagan holiday celebrations. (See? They're great!)

And thank you most of all to Maile, my co-author, fellow witch and fairy-finder. I love you.